LEYLAND ATLANTEANS

The Twilight Years

HOWARD WILDE

AMBERLEY

First published 2021

Amberley Publishing
The Hill, Stroud
Gloucestershire, GL5 4EP

www.amberley-books.com

Copyright © Howard Wilde, 2021

The right of Howard Wilde to be identified as
the Author of this work has been asserted in
accordance with the Copyrights, Designs and
Patents Act 1988.

ISBN 978 1 3981 0718 2 (print)
ISBN 978 1 3981 0719 9 (ebook)

British Library Cataloguing in Publication Data.
A catalogue record for this book is available from
the British Library.

Typesetting by SJmagic DESIGN SERVICES, India.
Printed in Great Britain.

Contents

Introduction

A Brief History

Ask bus enthusiasts of a senior age what they consider to be their classic double-deck bus design and many would probably suggest a version with the engine at the front, positioned over the front axle, with the driver divorced from the rest of the bus in a separate cab alongside the engine. Downstairs passengers would be seated behind a bulkhead partition directly behind the cab, tended to by a conductor who would collect fares, supervise loading and signal to the driver when to start or stop by means of a bell or buzzer. Access would likely be at the back, usually via an open platform – the classic 'back-loader', no less.

This layout may even be recalled with nostalgia by those with no dedicated interest in buses generally. They will reminisce fondly about 'those old buses with the door at the back that I used to go to school on'. Children's picture storybooks will depict the wheels on the bus that go round and round as belonging to something of that exact specification.

However, the fact is that, for many decades now, the main layout for a double-decker has been with the engine mounted at the back, with passengers boarding via a door directly alongside the driver.

Rear-engined double-deckers are nothing new, with examples built in the United States back in the 1930s. In the UK, it was Leyland Motors who took up the concept in the 1950s. Two prototypes of what was christened 'Lowloader' were built: STC 90 with a Saunders-Roe body in 1952; and Metro-Cammell-bodied XTC 684 in 1954. Both featured a small turbo-charged Leyland 0.350 engine mounted at the rear; but, despite that, the traditional layout was maintained. The door remained at the back and the driver remained in a separate cab. STF 90 had a trolleybus style full front, while XTC 684 had a half-cab layout.

Then, in 1956, the design changed radically. Aided by the recent legalisation of 30-foot-long double-deckers, Leyland worked in partnership with Metro-Cammell and produced 281 ATC. This was much more recognisable as the layout we know today, with the door alongside the driver, ahead of the front axle, and with a transversely mounted rear engine. This vehicle was exhibited at the Commercial Motor Show at Earl's Court that year and introduced the name 'Atlantean' to the public for the first time. The prototype was of semi-integral construction, with the Metro-Cammell body supporting the chassis structure. Leyland adopted the chassis designation PDR1, where 'PDR' denoted 'Passenger Double-deck Rear-engine'.

The first production Leyland Atlanteans appeared in 1958, by which time the semi-integral idea had been ditched and the model was a traditional separate chassis version. The engine was also moved from within the body structure to a separate compartment outside the lower saloon to reduce noise levels. This gave the Atlantean – and most competitors' models that followed – that distinctive 'bustle' at the back.

The initial production of Atlanteans were designated as type PDR1/1 and featured Leyland's 0.600 engine, together with Pneumocyclic semi-automatic transmission. The larger 0.680 engine was also offered as an option. The honour of being the first operator to put a production

Atlantean into regular service went to Wallasey Corporation, with their FHF 451 appropriately receiving fleet number 1.

It wasn't long before there was a rival to the Atlantean, when Daimler introduced its highly popular Fleetline model in 1960. The Fleetline also offered operators a true low-height option (13 feet 8 inches) with conventional seating on both decks, rather than the somewhat cumbersome lowbridge arrangement featured on most front-engined vehicles, with a sunken offside gangway and seating across the remaining width of the upper deck. The Atlantean, however, because of a conventional back axle downstairs, had to rely on a rather curious semi-lowbridge layout, featuring four rows of lowbridge-style seating towards the rear of the upper deck. Leyland later addressed this shortcoming in the PDR1/2 variant, utilising the rear axle arrangement from the front-engined low-height Albion Lowlander – Albion being a Leyland subsidiary by this time. There then followed a later PDR1/3 version. However, relatively few of either were produced.

A longer 33-foot version, designated PDR2/1, was introduced in 1967, taking advantage of a change in Construction and Use regulations. This further increased the Atlantean's carrying capacity and continued the drive towards driver-only, pay-as-you-board operation (legalised for double-deckers in 1966) and often employing a double-door layout with a front entrance and centre exit.

In 1972, Leyland introduced a revised Atlantean: the AN68 type, replacing the previous PDR versions. A wider entrance was provided. There were also some safety improvements, including an alarm to warn of engine overheating, a new parking brake and collision protection for the brake controls and steering box.

The Atlantean remained popular with many operators during the 1970s and 1980s, despite the growing presence of newer double-deckers from both Leyland's competitors – the likes of Scania, Dennis and MCW – and from Leyland itself, with its Titan and Olympian models. There was also the continuing availability of the Fleetline and Bristol's popular VR – both by this time under Leyland ownership and both ceasing production in the early 1980s.

The final UK Atlanteans were completed in 1984, with numerically the last chassis going to Lancaster in July that year. However, there were earlier chassis registered a few months after the Lancaster example, entering service with Blackpool, Fylde and Merseyside PTE. Production continued for a while for export models, before ending completely in 1986.

Thus, the Leyland Atlantean enjoyed an uninterrupted production run of nearly thirty years. Examples were built for independent operators, for corporation fleets, for London Transport, for the British Electric Traction fleets, for the National Bus Company subsidiaries, and for most of the PTE operators. There were also export sales all over the world. By the end of production, over 15,000 Atlanteans had been built.

Some Technical Details

In the photo captions in this book, I've referred to different types of Atlanteans by their chassis designation codes. I enclose a list of the ones featured for ease of reference.

PDR1/1: Leyland 0.600 engine, with 0.680 as option. 30 feet long. Pneumocyclic gearbox.
PDR1A/1: Leyland 0.680 engine, with 0.600 as option. Rationalised Pneumocyclic gearbox.
PDR2/1: As PDR1A/1, but 33 feet (10 metres in length). Leyland 0.680 engine only.
AN68 version: Replacement for PDR series. 0.680 engine as standard.

Later development variants as follows:
AN68A: Leyland G2 transmission.

AN68B: Leyland LVA45 automatic transmission. New fuel pump.

AN68C: As AN68B, but with semi-automatic gearbox.

AN68D: Rationalised 0.680 engine, featuring componentry employed in the later L11 and TL11 units.

Further figures identify the chassis length: '1' for 9.5 metre (30 feet), '2' for 10 metre (33 feet).

Right- and left-hand drive models are distinguished by 'R' or 'L' respectively. For example, 'AN68/1R' would denote a 9.5-metre, right-hand drive bus.

AN69 version: As per AN68, but with turbocharged 0.690 engine. Mainly for export models.

About This Book

This book concentrates on the Atlantean's twilight years: the period from the mid-1980s onwards. It features Atlanteans in the UK and Ireland of various types and with different owners, at work, at rest, or in preservation retirement.

Grateful thanks go to Graham Ashworth and Phil Halewood, for very kindly providing photographs and related background information. All other photographs not credited to them are my own, as are any opinions expressed throughout.

There have been several useful points of reference to help gather and verify facts, figures and general dates, including various 'G-list' publications of the PSV Circle; the excellent *Bus Lists on the Web* website; and the splendid *The Leyland Bus* by Doug Jack, published by Transport Publishing Company – truly the definitive record of all things Leyland.

I very much hope that you enjoy.

Howard Wilde,

July 2020

Double-deckers

Wigan Corporation purchased the first production AN68 Atlanteans, taking delivery of a batch of ten long wheelbase AN68/2R examples in 1972. These Northern Counties-bodied examples all passed to Greater Manchester PTE – along with the rest of the Wigan fleet – upon local government reorganisation in 1974. The very first of the batch – GMPTE 3330 (NEK 1K), originally Wigan 1 – is seen visiting the Manchester Museum of Transport in March 1985. It was apparently destined for preservation, but sadly this was not to be. However, similar NEK 9K was eventually restored to Wigan condition.

Famous Lincolnshire independent Delaine of Bourne operated No. 72 (ACT 540L) – a Northern Counties-bodied AN68/2R – from new in 1973. The company's trademark polished chrome beading is much in evidence in this view from July 1999, when No. 72 was a visitor to the Sandtoft Trolleybus Museum. Delaine has since retained it as a preserved heritage vehicle.

Remnants of Brighton Transport's livery are on show on OYJ 71R in the Sheffield Omnibus fleet, with the new operator's colours only added to half of the front end. This East Lancs-bodied AN68/1R had been new to the south coast municipal in December 1976. The brutal and decaying architecture on Pond Street in Sheffield forms a grim backdrop in this November 1992 view.

Angular Massey bodywork is fitted to this venerable PDR1/1 survivor. YWC 648F was new to Colchester in 1968 and was later converted by them to open-top layout. By the time of this view in October 2001, it was in service on city sightseeing tours in Liverpool with Reilly (Maghull Coaches) of Bootle. The bus was eventually exported to a museum in Thailand in 2013.

Another newer ex-Colchester Atlantean was TPU 69R – an AN68A/1R with ECW bodywork, new to the corporation in 1977. It is pictured later in life under Drawlane ownership, in their C-Line subsidiary, in central Manchester in October 1992.

Long wheelbase Northern Counties-bodied AN68C/2R VCX 340X was new to Longstaff of Mirfield in April 1982. In this view eleven years later, it was owned by another West Yorkshire independent, Black Prince of Morley. It is seen in The Headrow in Leeds, looking resplendent in their livery.

A one-off purchase for Bee Line in 1990 was YDS 651S – an Alexander-bodied AN68/1R that had been new to Grahams of Paisley in 1977. It was initially operated in its previous orange and cream livery before a repaint into Bee Line colours. In this view in central Manchester in May 1994, the Bee Line red and yellow are in the same proportions as the livery of fellow British Bus subsidiary, North Western.

Barrow Corporation bought four AN68D/1Rs with Northern Counties bodywork between 1983 and 1984. These were to a similar specification to those being delivered to Greater Manchester PTE. All later passed to Stagecoach's Ribble subsidiary, following Barrow's collapse in May 1989. LEO 734Y is seen with Sheffield Omnibus in their Preston-derived livery, in Sheffield in January 1995. The bus has since been preserved back to its original Barrow condition.

ASD 31T was an AN68A/1R with Alexander bodywork, new to A1 Co-operative member, Dunn of Stevenston in April 1979. It later passed to Blue Bus of Horwich and is seen with them in this view in Wigan bus station in February 1998.

Cleveland Transit undertook a refurbishment programme in the 1980s that saw twelve 1970 PDR1A/1 Atlanteans receive new Northern Counties bodies, replacing original bodywork by the same manufacturer. Eight of these were acquired by East Yorkshire in the early 1990s. In this April 1996 shot two examples lay over near Hull station, their original identities further obscured by Northern Ireland reregistrations. Nos 931 (FBZ 2931) and 933 (FBZ 2933) had originally been registered SXG 48H and SDC 143H respectively. Unusually, Fleetline engine cowls were deployed in the rebodying, as can be seen on No. 933.

ONN 571P started life as an ECW-bodied AN68/1R – one of a batch of seven delivered to Trent as their No. 571 in 1976. This was badly damaged in a depot fire when nearly new, along with two other buses that perished in the blaze. No. 571 was salvaged and rebodied by Willowbrook to their own standard design. The bus is pictured in Nottingham in January 1995, in use with Barton. This well-known name was by this time under Trent control, under the ownership of the larger Wellglade group.

Several Atlanteans that had been new to Aberdeen Corporation and its successor, Grampian, became popular second-hand purchases throughout Britain. Alexander-bodied AN68/1R NRG 158M is seen with Blue Bus of Horwich in Bolton in May 1991. The bus had been acquired by them from Lancaster.

Another Atlantean from the same 1973 batch as the previous Blue Bus example was Finglands No. 725 (NRG 168M). This also had seen service with Lancaster prior to acquisition. The bus is captured, laying over on football duties in Chorlton Street, Manchester, in July 1992.

East Midland No. 436 (KSA 189P) was an Alexander-bodied AN68A/1R that had been new to Grampian in 1976. It is pictured in York Street, Manchester, in June 1989. The Frontrunner identity carried was adopted by East Midland for operations outside their regular geographical area.

First made an extremely long-distance inter-group cascade when it transferred Alexander-bodied Atlanteans from Aberdeen to Devon and Cornwall in the early 2000s. Red Bus 1009 (URS 327X) – an AN68C/1R, new to Grampian in 1982 – is pictured in the small bus station in Ilfracombe, Devon, in June 2001. The bus's destination – Westwood Ho! – is the only UK place name to feature an exclamation mark, being named after a Charles Kingsley novel.

Another former – and much older – Aberdeen Atlantean to make the long trek to Devon was GRS 114E. This Alexander-bodied PDR1 was new to the corporation in 1967, being converted to open-top later in life. A beautiful sunny day In Woolacombe in June 2001 sees it in use on a regular shuttle service with Lancaster Leisure, owners of the nearby Woolacombe Bay Holiday Parcs.

This view in Accrington in September 1990 shows Blackburn Transport No. 111 (PCW 111P), carrying a commemorative heritage livery, complete with intricate lining-out. This East Lancs-bodied AN68A/1R from 1976 would later end up in service with MTL Manchester.

A fairly late Blackburn Atlantean – East Lancs-bodied AN68D/1R, No. 24 (FCK 24Y) – is captured in the town's bus station in November 1992. The bus was new to them in July 1983.

Lancaster owned two former Blackburn East Lancs-bodied AN68/1Rs that they had converted to open-top layout. Of these, No. 87 (UBV 87L) is pictured in Morecambe in June 1993. Lancaster's operations were taken over by Stagecoach several months later.

Former Blackburn JFR No. 398N – a 1975 AN68/1R with East Lancs body – is pictured in the bright yellow and white livery of Stuart of Hyde. The photograph was taken in Ashton-under-Lyne bus station in August 1990.

The proximity of famous independent operator Fishwick to the Leyland works resulted in several interesting acquisitions over the years. One such vehicle was GRN 895W. The chassis was new in 1975 as the prototype AN69 Atlantean, powered by Leyland's turbocharged 0.690 engine. It was used by Leyland to develop noise-reduction innovations that later found their way into the last of London Transport's Leyland Fleetlines – the B20 project. Fishwick purchased the chassis in 1980 and had it bodied by ECW, with it entering service in 1981. The distinctive rear engine styling that also appeared on those B20 Fleetlines is visible in this view of the depot yard in April 1991.

Fishwick acquired a second AN69 from Leyland, which entered service in 1984. This was A462 LFV – an AN69/2L left-hand drive model that had been converted to right-hand drive. It was also the only Atlantean to carry ECW's Leyland Olympian-style bodywork. It is seen near Preston Bus's garage in September 1998. Fishwick's AN69 Atlanteans were the only examples to see service in the UK. Both are currently preserved.

Slightly more mundane Atlantean purchases by Fishwick were three East Lancs-bodied AN68s, delivered between 1974 and 1976. Two of these – SRN 103P and XTB 729N – are pictured at Fishwick's Leyland depot in April 1991.

Representative of the large number of Northern Counties-bodied Atlanteans delivered to SELNEC and Greater Manchester PTEs over the years is No. 7762 (UNA 762S). This view in central Manchester in March 1994 captures it in service with GM Buses North, although the previous GM Buses name is still displayed. The bus is unusual in being one of a batch that had been sold to Yorkshire Rider at deregulation, but which GM North then bought back to bolster fleet strength upon their formation.

In addition to Northern Counties, Park Royal also built bodywork for the SELNEC and Greater Manchester fleets. Captured later in life with GM Buses South is No. 7862 (UNA 862S), seen in Piccadilly, Manchester, in January 1996. This AN68A/1R had been new to GMPTE in December 1977.

Another Park Royal-bodied ex-GM Atlantean from the same batch as the previous photo is UNA 862S, pictured in Lincoln in October 1996. The operator is a local company, Eagre of Gainsborough. The name 'Eagre' refers to a tidal bore, in this instance seen occasionally on the nearby River Trent.

A faithful old soldier from corporation days. Metro-Cammell-bodied PDR1/1, DBA 227C was new to Salford Corporation in 1965. Following transfer to SELNEC PTE and later Greater Manchester PTE, it was then sold to Lancaster along with others from the same batch. A conversion to open-top followed later. It was then sold to Fylde and became a familiar sight in and around Blackpool for many more years. A colourful No. 89, complete with an unusual partial glass cover (added by Fylde), is seen working the Coastliner promenade service in Blackpool in May 1990.

GM Buses No. 8620 (ANA 620Y) is pictured in Piccadilly bus station in Manchester in September 1988, carrying branding for Route 50. This Northern Counties-bodied AN68D/1R is typical of the later Atlanteans purchased by predecessor, Greater Manchester PTE. It had been new to them in February 1983.

Ribble obtained various second-hand double-deckers as they expanded their operations at deregulation. Among these were some former GMPTE AN68/1Rs with Park Royal bodies. Here 1642 (VNB 167L) – new to SELNEC in 1973 – is pictured in Mosley Street, Manchester, in October 1989. However, despite appearances to the contrary, the bus is no longer a Ribble vehicle in this view, having been transferred to Bee Line Buzz Company. This was a result of the deal at the time between Ribble's owner, Stagecoach, and Drawlane Group, which saw Stagecoach relinquish their Manchester operations.

Merseyside operator Gemsam (Liverbus) of Huyton commenced operations with a batch of former GM Standard Atlanteans. A very smart Northern Counties-bodied AN68A/1R, ONF 678R, is pictured at work in central Liverpool in April 1991.

Bolton Moor Lane bus station in July 1991 and a rather careworn Ribble 1665 (JVM 989N) loads passengers bound for Rochdale. This former GMPTE AN68/1R with Northern Counties body had come to Ribble via fellow Stagecoach subsidiary, East Midland.

Stott of Oldham ANC 932T is pictured at work in Oldham town centre in January 1996. This Park Royal-bodied AN68A/1R had been new to GMPTE in 1979. Stott's acquired it in 1995 from A1 Service member Brown of Dreghorn. Prior to that it had seen service just a few miles south of Oldham with Pennine Blue.

A former GMPTE Northern Counties-bodied AN68D/1R, transferred by owners First to West Yorkshire and the First Huddersfield fleet. No. 6452 (A737 NNA) carries First's 'Barbie 2' corporate livery – a livery not seen on similar Atlanteans while in Manchester. It also sports a replacement West Yorkshire PTE-style destination display, as it leaves Huddersfield bus station in April 2002.

One of the last places in Britain to see Atlanteans on daily frontline service was Birmingham, thanks to North Birmingham Busways. This independent started operations in 1994, adopting Blackpool livery, following their initial purchase of a batch of ex-Blackpool Atlanteans. Former GMPTE Northern Counties-bodied AN68D/1R A657 HNB is captured in the same colours, in central Birmingham in October 2006, still looking sprightly for a twenty-three-year-old bus.

Blackpool favoured the longer Atlantean for their double-deck requirements, taking examples from 1977 to 1984. Here 1983 AN68D/2R 355 (A355 HHG) is pictured in Talbot Road in the town in May 1990. The specified East Lancs bodywork managed to accommodate a substantial eighty-six seated passengers.

Some of Blackpool's Atlanteans had long lives within the resort. No. 329 (URN 329V) – a 1979 AN68A/2R with East Lancs body – is pictured near the town's North Pier in October 2001, working the seafront Service 1 to St Annes.

Blackpool's final Atlanteans were a pair of East Lancs-bodied AN68D/2Rs, new in September 1984 and featuring coach seats. The first of the two – No. 363 (B363 UBV) – is seen just off the seafront in June 1994.

Blue Bus of Horwich acquired several former Blackpool Atlanteans. In this shot their No. 34 (JFV 314S) is pictured in Deansgate, Bolton, in August 1992. The AN68A/2R was new to Blackpool in July 1978.

Irish state-owned transport operator Córas Iompair Éireann (CIE) was a major Atlantean customer from the mid-1960s through to the end of the 1970s. Their final examples were 238 AN68/1R and AN68A/1R models, fitted with Van Hool McArdle bodywork – a joint venture between the Belgian Van Hool and Irish Thomas McArdle, building buses at the former CIE works at Spa Road in Dublin. No. DF791 (791 BIK) is seen later in life with Dublin Bus in August 1991. The 'F' in the fleet number denoted a replacement DAF engine – a sign of the general souring of relationships between CIE and Leyland over the years.

Before the AN68s, there were PDR1/1 and PDR1A/1 models, fitted with a highly distinctive body style, built by CIE themselves on Metal Sections frames. CIE ended up being the last operator to put new PDR1A Atlanteans into service, with the last ones new in early 1975. The final examples were in fact bodied by Van Hool McArdle to the previous CIE/Metal Sections design. This included what eventually became Dublin Bus DF583 (583 ZU), pictured in Dublin's O'Connell Street in August 1991. Once again, a DAF engine has replaced a Leyland one.

Over in Northern Ireland, Ulsterbus No. 924 (COI 924) was an example of a batch of forty Alexander Belfast-bodied PDR2/1s, new between 1971 and 1973. It is pictured, withdrawn from service, at Ulsterbus's Larne garage in August 1991.

Fylde No. 77 (ATD 281J) was one of three PDR1A/1s with Northern Counties bodywork that had been new to Fylde's predecessor, Lytham St Annes Corporation, in 1970. In this May 1988 view, No. 77 is captured turning out of Talbot Road in Blackpool. The Blue Buses name, adopted by Fylde after deregulation, is carried above the destination display. This vehicle enjoyed a long life on the Fylde coast, remaining in use until 1996 before passing into preservation.

Fylde had a number of their 1970s Atlanteans rebuilt and refurbished by original bodybuilder Northern Counties in the early 1990s. AN68A/1R 72 – reregistered with the ageless Northern Ireland mark OJI 4372 – had been new as No. 86 (EBV 86S) in December 1977. The bus is captured at Squires Gate with the Fylde garage in the background, in September 1993.

Fylde took delivery of six AN68/1R Atlanteans in 1975. The bodywork was originally to be by Willowbrook, but the work was sub-contracted by them to Northern Counties, with Willowbrook doing some finishing work to what were essentially standard NCME bodies. The buses carried body numbers from both companies as a result. Fylde No. 83 (HRN 103N) passes South Shore in this view from September 1993.

Four Atlanteans that had been new to Eastbourne in 1975 found their way into the Warrington fleet at the start of the 1990s. Warrington used them in a special Mid-Cheshire Bus Lines unit, for which the previous operator's livery was retained. East Lancs-bodied AN68/1R 108 (GHC 522N) is pictured in the town in May 1990.

Rather elderly purchases for Citibus in Manchester in 1988 were three PDR1A/1s with East Lancs bodies that had been new to Eastbourne in 1972. They came to Citibus from People's Provincial. Citibus No.816 (KHC 816K) is pictured in Piccadilly bus station in Manchester in July 1990.

Another Eastbourne Atlantean (from the same batch as the previous Citibus example) was KHC 813K. In February 1996, it was in service as an open-topper with Guide Friday in their home town of Stratford-upon-Avon.

Rossendale No. 136 (CJK 36V) is pictured waiting at the lights on Oldham Street in central Manchester in June 1991. This was one of six East Lancs-bodied AN68A/1Rs that were originally new to Eastbourne. They were purchased by Rossendale from Topline Buses in Hastings – a venture in whom Eastbourne originally had a stake, before selling their share to Stagecoach.

Lincolnshire Road Car No. 732 (YJK 932V) was an East Lancs-bodied AN68A/2R, new to Eastbourne in 1979. It came to Road Car from Sheffield Omnibus as an inter-group transfer by Traction Group – parent company of both operators at the time. No. 732 passes alongside the bus station in Lincoln in this view from October 1996.

Lothian and its predecessor Edinburgh Corporation were loyal Atlantean customers from the 1960s through to the early 1980s. Lothian No. 618 (OSC 618V) from 1979 demonstrates the classic Alexander body, in this case with panoramic windows and double doors. The bus is pictured on a sunny August morning in 1994, heading along Edinburgh's York Place.

Another similar, but slightly older, Alexander-bodied AN68A/1R for Lothian was No. 534 (SSG 534R), new to them in 1976. Lothian's classic madder and white livery (inherited from Edinburgh Corporation days) is shown off to good advantage in this rainy view in the city in 1994.

Lothian No. 44 (BFS 44L) – named *Gaelic Star* – was one of several 1973 Alexander-bodied AN68/1Rs converted to open-top for city tour work, primarily in competition with Guide Friday. The Royal Mile in Edinburgh's Old Town is the location for this August 1994 view.

ATL-owned SUT of Sheffield acquired a batch of former Edinburgh Corporation Alexander-bodied PDR1A/1s from Lothian in the early deregulation years. WFS 290K is pictured with SUT in Pond Street in Sheffield in October 1988. It had been new in the Scottish capital in 1972.

Other Edinburgh Atlanteans from the same batch as the SUT example were acquired by North Western. No. 485 (WFS 261K) is pictured in Lever Street bus station in Manchester in October 1989, laying over on the No. 292 service that served Trafford Park.

Several National Bus Company subsidiaries took delivery of Atlanteans to a similar design during the 1970s and early 1980s, with bodywork either by Park Royal or Roe – Leyland and the two bodybuilders all being part of British Leyland at the time. One such operator was Ribble, who took delivery of 104 Park Royal-bodied examples between 1974 and 1976. No. 1402 (NRN 402P) – an AN68/1R, new in 1976 – is pictured with post-NBC, management-owned Ribble in Barrow-in-Furness in March 1988.

Another Ribble Atlantean was RTF 636M, which was new to them in 1974. It is pictured with Sheffield independent Sheafline, parked near the city's railway station in September 1989. The bus had come to them from Drawlane-owned North Western. This was during a period when Drawlane was linked with a plan to buy Sheafline out, which in the end came to nothing.

The first NBC-spec Atlanteans were delivered to London Country in 1972. These were ninety Park Royal-bodied dual-door vehicles, all designated PDR1A/1 Special – a variant that featured some of the new elements of the forthcoming AN68 model. JPL 141K is seen here in service with West Yorkshire independent Black Prince of Morley in Leeds in June 1990. The bus came from London Country North West – one of the companies formed when London Country was split into four parts in 1986. LCNW's NBC-style livery is still carried.

Aston Express of Killamarsh UPK 132S was another former London Country Park Royal-bodied Atlantean – this time a later AN68A/1R model from 1978. The bus is pictured at a bus rally at Sheffield's Meadowhall shopping centre in September 1992. The London Transport-style blind layout – part of which has been painted over by Aston – had been fitted retrospectively by earlier owner EnsignBus. Note also the traditional Leyland badge.

Hulme Hall Coaches MUA 969P waits over in Hyde bus station in October 1990, working one of the company's commercially registered school services to the school of the same name in Cheadle Hulme. This AN68/1R was new to NBC operator Yorkshire Woollen in 1976. Its body was built by Roe, using parts originating from Park Royal.

ECW also bodied large numbers of Atlanteans for NBC fleets. Former Ribble TRN 469V is pictured under Stagecoach group ownership with Cumberland – branded as CMS Carlislebus – on English Street in Carlisle in May 1991. This AN68A/1R example had been new in January 1980.

Rhodes of Wawne was running this ECW-bodied AN68/1R in Hull in August 1992. JJG 7P had been new to East Kent in 1976 – one of a batch fifteen such buses. Rhodes sold out to East Yorkshire shortly after this photograph was taken.

Bee Line No. 628 (LCD 42P) was a former Southdown Roe-bodied AN68/1R, pictured exiting Newton Street in Manchester in June 1991. This bus was nearly sixteen years old in this view, having been new in December 1975.

Trent's attractive deregulation livery of red and silver is carried by their No. 577 (LRB 577W) in this view in Derby in August 1991. This AN68C/1R with ECW bodywork was one of eight and was new to the company in 1981.

Citibus of Chadderton purchased four former Southdown AN68/1Rs with Park Royal bodies for further service. Their No. 139 (SUF 139N) is pictured on High Street in Manchester in September 1991. Tram tracks for Manchester's Metrolink are in place alongside the bus, in readiness for the commencement of services the following year.

MPT 311P was one of a batch of dual-doored ECW-bodied AN68/1Rs that had been new to Northern General in 1975. In this view in Hull in August 1992, it is in service with East Yorkshire. The centre door has been blocked off in a rather rudimentary conversion.

Gateshead Metro interchange in May 1993, and VFM Buses No. 3545 (MBR 445T) is departing with a healthy load towards Fellgate Estate. This ECW-bodied AN68A/1R had been new to Northern General in 1979. VFM Buses (short for 'value for money') was the trading name for Tyneside Omnibus Company, a former subsidiary of Northern General that was resurrected after deregulation by the parent Go Ahead Group.

Another VFM Atlantean and another one that had also been new to Northern General. No. 3483 (AUP 383W) was a Roe-bodied AN68B/1R from 1980. In this view it is captured on Market Street East in Newcastle in May 1993.

Captured on a sunny day in South John Street, Liverpool, in June 1992 is Liverline No. 73 (XPG 159T). This AN68A/1R with Park Royal body had been new to London Country in 1978.

A former East Yorkshire AN68/1R with Park Royal body, captured in service with Metro of Hull in August 1992. It appears that a reputation for speed is being celebrated, as PAT 951M is named *Gonzales* in this view – as in Speedy Gonzales, the famous Warner Brothers cartoon character.

From the same batch as *Gonzales* was No. 952 (TIJ 952), still in service with East Yorkshire on the same day as the previous photo. This had originally been PAT 952M and was selected by East Yorkshire for a refurbishment project in 1989, with a view to extending vehicle service life. Noticeable features were a new front grille and electronic destination display. No. 952 then gained the cherished plate the following year. The renovated bus remained a one-off, however, lasting in service until 1996.

Timeline Travel No. 121 (RFR 411P) was an ECW-bodied AN68/1R that had been new to Ribble in 1976. It is pictured crossing from Victoria Bridge Street into Cateaton Street in Manchester in March 1994. Sadly, the bus was later written off following upper-deck fire damage, sustained while working a schools contract.

In 1990, Yorkshire Rider acquired nine former London Country Roe-bodied AN68B/1Rs, complementing similar Atlanteans of their own. No. 6430 (KPJ 261W) is seen near the Corn Exchange in central Leeds in April 1996. By this time Yorkshire Rider was owned by First Group, with the Leeds operation branded Leeds CityLink.

Ulsterbus open-topper No. 2904 (OXI 514) is pictured operating the tourist service to Ben Crom reservoir within the beautiful Silent Valley in Northern Ireland, in September 1993. This ECW-bodied AN68A/1R had been new to Yorkshire Woollen as JYG 416V in 1979. Conversion to open-top took place after acquisition by Ulsterbus, along with the addition of a nearside wheelchair lift.

Sandhurst of Leicester was operating TRT 96M on rail replacement duties in this view outside New Street Station in Birmingham in April 1992. This Roe-bodied AN68/1R had been new to Ipswich Corporation in 1974.

A slightly later former Ipswich Roe-bodied Atlantean was RDX 13R – an AN68A/1R that had been new to them in 1976. It is pictured in Lincoln bus station in October 1996, by this time owned by Lincolnshire Road Car as their No. 1323. The nearside view reveals a conversion to single-door.

East Lancs-bodied AN68A/1R RGV 40W is seen here with Hyndburn as their No. 135. The bus had been new to Ipswich in 1980. Passengers board at Moor Lane bus station in Bolton in this view from August 1992, bound for Accrington on Service 500.

LDX 75G is pictured with Chepstow Classic Coaches, visiting the Scottish Vintage Bus Museum at Lathalmond in August 2018. This ECW-bodied PDR1/1 was new to Ipswich Corporation in 1968. It also saw service in the interim with Eastbourne, who had it converted to open-top in the 1980s.

The distinctive – even eccentric – style of bodywork specified by Nottingham over the years is well demonstrated by No. 546 (OTO 546M), pictured in Old Market Square in the city in November 1991. East Lancs built the body on this AN68/1R, which was new in January 1974. At the time, this was one of the older vehicles still in service with Nottingham.

Also bodying buses to the distinctive Nottingham design were Northern Counties. Nottingham No. 667 (XTV 667S) – a 1978 AN68A/1R – passes the now-demolished Broadmarsh bus station in the city centre in October 1992.

Slightly more off-the-peg Atlanteans for Nottingham were ten Roe-bodied AN68C/1R models, new in 1981. Nottingham's preferred HELP front bumpers were featured, together with the operator's desire to maximise seating capacity – eighty seats being accommodated in a design that would normally only carry seventy-five at most. Nottingham No. 480 (NNN 480W) is seen in the city in October 1992.

Mybus of Hadfield GVO 713N is captured, parked up in Lever Street bus station in Manchester in July 1992. This former Nottingham East Lancs-bodied AN68/1R still carries the unusual livery of the council company Boro'line Maidstone, who had gone out of business several months earlier.

A large number of Nottingham double-deckers enjoyed a subsequent life all over the country and abroad with Guide Friday – mainly as open-toppers. East Lancs-bodied AN68/1R OTO 584M is pictured on the Royal Mile in Edinburgh's old town in August 1994.

Hull No. 361 (GAT 200N) – a 1975 AN68/1R with Roe bodywork – takes centre stage in this view near the city's railway station in August 1992. Alongside is sister vehicle No. 364 (GAT 203N), while an older PDR1A/1, No. 317 (ARH 317K), waits behind.

'On hire to railways' proclaims the blind in the destination box of WAG 372X of Happy Al's of Birkenhead, as it participates in Merseyrail replacement services in this shot in James Street, Liverpool, in August 1995. This Roe-bodied AN68C/1R was one of fifteen new to Hull in 1982.

After deregulation Fylde purchased several second-hand double-deckers, including a significant number of Atlanteans from Hull. Roe-bodied PDR1A/1 ARH 304K, new in 1972, was photographed on Blackpool Promenade in June 1992, decked out in a very bright blue and yellow livery.

An older former Hull Atlantean was PRH 257G. This PDR1A/1 with an earlier style of Roe body was new in 1969. It is seen in service as an open-topper with Guide Friday in Stratford-upon-Avon in February 1996.

Both Merseybus and previous Merseyside PTE identities are visible in this view of a rather down-at-heel No. 1834 (WWM 917W) in Lime Street in Liverpool in May 1990. This East Lancs-bodied AN68A/1R had been new to the PTE ten years previously. It still wears the PTE-inspired livery in this picture.

Merseybus No. 1807 (PKA 721S) powers along the Strand in Liverpool in April 1991, with part of the famous Liver Building visible in the background. This AN68A/1R had bodywork by MCW and was new to Merseyside PTE in 1978. Both it and the Alexander-bodied Atlantean following carry the attractive maroon and cream livery, introduced by Merseybus in the late 1980s.

Merseyside PTE purchased large numbers of Alexander-bodied Atlanteans in the 1970s and 1980s, of which Merseybus No. 1527 (GKA 527M) was typical. This 1973 AN68/1R was captured heading out of Water Street in Liverpool in April 1991.

Similar Merseybus No. 1524 (GKA 524M) was converted to open-top following fire damage in 1983. It is pictured working the open-top circular tour in Southport in June 1991. This had been a long-standing attraction in the town, going back to Southport Corporation days, reflected by the retention of Southport livery by both Merseyside PTE and Merseybus.

Relatively unusual bodywork by Willowbrook was specified by Merseyside PTE for thirty AN68B/1Rs, purchased between 1980 and 1982. Of these, No. 1847 (WWM 924W) was rendered more unusual still by MPTE's successor, Merseybus, who chose it for conversion to *The Merseymaid*, for use on cross-river services via the Mersey tunnels. A thorough refurbishment was carried out by MTL Engineering, featuring a new front grille, electronic destination display and the fitting of coach seats. No. 1824 is captured turning into Castle Street in Liverpool in June 1992.

WWM 932W demonstrates the original configuration of Merseyside PTE's Willowbrook-bodied Atlanteans while under the subsequent ownership of South Manchester of Hyde. The location is Mosley Street, Manchester, in December 1994.

Merseybus No.1758 (MTJ 758S) pauses on James Street in Liverpool in this August 1995 view. This East Lancs-bodied AN68A/1R, new in 1977, wears the later livery adopted across various MTL group fleets. There is also evidence – from the faded fleet name – of recent operation with MTL Manchester, before a return to home turf.

Having bought Alexander-bodied Atlanteans in the 1970s, Merseyside PTE returned to the combination later in the 1980s. What by this time was Merseybus No. 1952 (ACM 752X) – an AN68C/1R from 1982 – is seen in MTL group colours in Liverpool in February 1996.

Former Merseyside MCW-bodied AN68A/1R, PKA 725S, wears the smart red and white livery of Cartmell (Border) of Burnley as it enters the town's bus station in October 1994.

A Liverpool veteran brought back to the city's streets by Merseyside independent Forrest (Blue Triangle) of Bootle. Alexander-bodied PDR2/1 50 (XKC 861K) had been new to Merseyside PTE in December 1971, the result of an order placed previously by Liverpool Corporation. Parent, toddler and buggy are safely deposited in this view in Liverpool's Whitechapel in November 1993.

Citibus purchased NDR 508J in 1988. It was their first double-decker in a previously all-single-deck fleet. This Park Royal-bodied PDR2/1 had been new to Plymouth Corporation in 1971. Citibus acquired it from Lancashire operator Tyrer of Trawden and ran it for a time in Tyrer's livery, which was not dissimilar to their own. It is seen as such, parked up in Citibus's garage in Bradford, Manchester, in November 1988.

Plymouth bought fifteen AN68/1Rs with Park Royal dual-door bodies to NBC specification in 1975. What had been their No. 215 (GDR 215N) is seen fifteen years later with Liverline in Liverpool in May 1990. By this time the bus had been converted to single-door.

Finglands No. 1734 (LTK 96R) is pictured on Mosley Street in Manchester in October 1992. This was another ex-Plymouth Atlantean – this time a Roe-bodied AN68A/1R, which was new in 1977. Like the previous Liverline example, this bus started out life with two doors. It came to Finglands from Hyndburn.

With one of Scarborough's famous funicular cliff lifts – the St Nicholas Cliff Lift – in the background, Appleby's WJY 760 is pictured on open-top service duties on a glorious July day in 1997. This Metro-Cammell bodied PDR1/1 had been new to Plymouth in 1962, and was converted by them to open-top in 1976.

Another Atlantean from the same batch is WJY 758, in service with Keighley Bus Museum in June 2008, on a heritage summer service linking Bolton Abbey with the nearby station and related steam railway. The bus was sold the following year and moved back to Plymouth for continued preservation.

Captured in Sheffield in January 1995 is Sheffield Omnibus No. 1348 (CPO 348W). This AN68A/1R with East Lancs body was new to Portsmouth Corporation in 1980. When new, the bus had a separate entrance and centre exit.

Earlier Portsmouth Atlanteans had been Alexander-bodied AN68/1R examples, new in 1975. Five of these ended up with Shearings, including their No. 141 (HOR 310N), pictured in Barnsley in January 1991 during a fairly short-lived venture into South Yorkshire. They would later pass to Timeline, along with the rest of Shearings' local bus operations, following the company's decision to concentrate on their coaching business.

Preston No. 122 (CRN 122S) is captured loading passengers, bound for Lea, on Friargate in the town in September 1990. This AN68A/2R from 1977 had dual-door bodywork by East Lancs, with seats for eighty-two passengers.

North Western bought six from a batch of ten Alexander-bodied Atlanteans from Preston soon after deregulation. These AN68/2R examples had been new between late 1974 and early 1975. North Western No. 493 (GBV 103N) pulls away from the stand on Parker Street in Manchester in this view from July 1990.

Preston took further Alexander-bodied Atlanteans, with a batch of ten arriving in March 1980. These were AN68A/2R models, once again featuring Preston's preferred dual-door layout. No. 149 (UHG 149V) is seen alongside the Guildhall in April 1991.

Preston No. 176 (DRN 176Y) – an East Lancs-bodied AN68D/2R, new in 1983 – received the previous corporation crimson livery in 1998, in readiness for commemorations of the 120th anniversary of tram and bus operation in Preston the following year. It is pictured outside the Leyland Museum in September 1998 at a rally celebrating the 40th anniversary of the first production Atlantean.

South Yorkshire Transport No. 1698 (CWG 698V) was new to the predecessor PTE fleet in 1979. This Alexander-bodied AN68A/1R is seen in Sheffield's transport interchange in October 1990. Fifty of SYPTE's later Atlanteans, including this one, were unusual in featuring Voith D851 automatic gearboxes rather than Leyland's standard transmission option. Such a specification gave them a sound all of their own.

Manchester independent Citibus took large numbers of former South Yorkshire Atlanteans of various types in the late 1980s. East Lancs-bodied AN68A/1R 190 (UDT 190S) is pictured dropping off passengers in Ashton bus station in April 1991.

Tame Valley of Hyde commenced operations in 1991 with two former SYPTE Roe-bodied AN68A/1Rs. One of these – No. 57 (XWG 657T) – is pictured at rest in Stockport in June that year. Both vehicles received an in-house conversion to single-door.

Marshall double-deck bodywork was never very commonplace; and the only examples on Atlantean chassis were thirty AN68B/1R models, new to South Yorkshire PTE in 1981. South Yorkshire Transport No. 1823 (JKW 323W) is pictured in Sheffield city centre in May 1992.

Captured at the entrance to South Yorkshire Transport's Rotherham garage in August 1993 is their converted open-topper, No. 287 (SWB 287L) – an AN68/1R with Alexander body that was new to Sheffield in 1973. No. 287 carries SYT's bright Mainline identity and livery, as it performs shuttle duties to an open day at the depot. The bus has since been preserved to its original Sheffield condition, regaining a roof in the process.

South Yorkshire Transport No. 1752 (CWG 752V) heads along Pond Street in Sheffield in full Mainline livery in September 1993. This AN68A/1R with Roe bodywork had been new to the previous PTE fleet in 1979.

From the same batch as No. 1752 in the previous picture is CWG 769V, pictured with Guide Friday on Waverley Bridge in Edinburgh in August 1994. The bus is in use on an airport shuttle service, run in direct competition with the incumbent operator, Lothian.

CWG 730V was an AN68A/1R with Alexander body, new to South Yorkshire PTE in 1980. Subsequent disposal saw it owned by OK Travel of Bishop Auckland. It is seen emerging from underneath Newcastle's Eldon Square shopping centre in October 1995.

Looking immaculate in the highly traditional livery of Warstone Motors (Green Bus Services) of Great Wyrley is UET 678S. This was another former SYPTE Alexander-bodied AN68A/1R, this time new in 1978. As in the previous photo, this example has received a single-door conversion. The picture was taken in Wolverhampton in April 1996.

Rossendale No. 27 (SND 27X) was an AN68C/1R with East Lancs body, new in 1982. In 1986 the bus was converted to coach seats. The refurbishment also included the repositioning of the offside emergency exit door, which is visible in this view in Rawtenstall in March 1990. The original peaked roof dome had also been replaced by a later unit by this time due to roof damage.

Another Rossendale East Lancs-bodied Atlantean and another replaced front dome. This time it's slightly older No. 23 (ABN 723V), an AN68A/1R new in 1979. The photo was taken in Bolton in June 1998, with No. 23 arriving on the No. 273 from Burnley, its destination already set for the return journey.

Newcastle Central station in May 1993 forms the backdrop for Busways No. 251 (SCN 251S). Busways was formed at Deregulation to take over the bus operations of Tyne and Wear PTE. No. 251, an Alexander-bodied AN68A/2R, had been new to the PTE in 1978.

Demonstrating the unusual preference for nearside staircases – a specification going back to late Newcastle Corporation days – is Busways No. 543 (MVK 543R), operating in their Blue Bus Services division. This 1976 Alexander-bodied AN68A/2R had been new to Tyne and Wear PTE and was one of the later ones to feature this layout. The photo shows No. 543 on Market Street in Newcastle in May 1993, passing the local Northern Electric electricity showroom – very much a feature of days gone by.

Northern General No. 3525 (EJR 125W) is pictured at Gateshead Metro interchange in May 1993. This AN68C/2R with Alexander body had been new to Tyne and Wear PTE in 1981. It was one of ten of the batch that were transferred immediately to Northern General, never seeing service with the PTE.

A survivor from Newcastle Corporation days. SVK 627G is a 1969 PDR1/1 with Alexander bodywork, and was one of the earlier examples with a nearside staircase. It was subsequently converted to open-top and single-door by Tyne and Wear PTE. It is pictured with Chepstow Classic Coaches, visiting Lathalmond in August 2018.

Portland Street, Manchester, in August 1998, and former Tyne and Wear AVK 177V is in service with Finglands as their No. 1757. This Alexander-bodied AN68A/2R had been new eighteen years earlier.

Warrington purchased Atlanteans with East Lancs bodywork in several batches during the 1970s. Their No. 8 (XTB 8T) – an AN68A/1R, new in 1978 – is pictured on Buttermarket Street in the town in April 1990.

Leeds City Transport specified distinctive dual-door Roe bodywork on long-wheelbase Atlanteans and Fleetlines from the late 1960s into the 1970s. These all passed to West Yorkshire PTE, including some delivered new to the PTE from the original Leeds order. SUG 562M – a 1974 AN68/2R – is seen with WYPTE's deregulation successor, Yorkshire Rider, in Leeds Central bus station in June 1990.

A slightly older Leeds 'Jumbo' was JUG 514L, owned by Black Prince of Morley in this view on Vicar Lane in Leeds in September 1990. This AN68/2R, looking immaculate in Black Prince's attractive livery, had been new to the corporation in February 1973.

West Yorkshire PTE specified a more restrained Roe body style for their Atlantean purchases. This is demonstrated by 1974 AN68/1R 6005 (GUG 535N), captured in service with Yorkshire Rider in Leeds in April 1996. The First Group logo and Leeds CityLink name reflects Rider's owners at the time.

Later Roe-bodied Atlanteans in the WYPTE fleet had a higher windscreen and driving position. Here No. 6282 (PUA 282W) – an AN68C/1R, new in 1981 – is pictured with Yorkshire Rider in Huddersfield in April 1996. By this time No. 6282 carries First Group logos and the Kingfisher identity adopted by them for Huddersfield-area operations.

An acquisition by Chesterfield Transport from Yorkshire Rider. Roe-bodied AN68A/1R SUA 123R had been new to West Yorkshire PTE in 1977. The photo was taken in May 1994 at the Heart of the Pennines rally in Halifax.

Hyndburn No. 184 (JBV 820N) is pictured, looking rather in need of some TLC, in central Manchester in April 1989. The pre-deregulation livery style of the former borough council is still carried on this 1975 East Lancs-bodied AN68/1R – right down to the coat of arms. No. 184 was on hire to Wild (Central Coaches) of Oldham at the time.

A newer Hyndburn Atlantean was No. 198 (DBV 198W), seen here in the depot yard in Accrington in November 1992. This East Lancs-bodied AN68B/1R had been new in 1980 and was converted to open-top in the early 1990s.

All the sevens: Pennine Blue No. 7777 (PHG 777P) is pictured in Warrington Street, Ashton-under-Lyne, in October 1992. This East Lancs-bodied AN68/1R had been new to Hyndburn as their No. 186 in February 1976. It came to Pennine Blue from Merseyside independent operator C & M Travel of Aintree.

Atlantean variety in the fleet of Liverline in Liverpool in May 1990. On the left is East Lancs-bodied AN68A/1R 50 (URN 327R). This at the time was on long-term loan from Hyndburn and was subsequently purchased outright. On the right is No. 11 (JGA 192N) – one of the batch of ex-Greater Glasgow AN68/1Rs with Alexander bodies with which Liverline originally commenced operations.

The Atlantean loomed large in Glasgow, with 1,449 examples purchased by Glasgow Corporation and successors Greater Glasgow and Strathclyde PTEs, from the start of production until the early 1980s. By 1988, the oldest Atlantean in the Strathclyde Transport fleet was Alexander-bodied AN68/1R LA664 (HGD 870L), pictured in Argyle Street in the city in that year. New in 1973, the bus received former Glasgow Corporation livery in 1994 to commemorate the corporation's centenary. Earmarked for preservation, it was unfortunately scrapped in error. (Courtesy of Phil Halewood)

Typical of Glasgow Atlanteans in the later years were the Alexander-bodied examples with panoramic windows. Of these, 1970s examples numbered between LA751 and LA1051 were disposed of prematurely in the 1980s over structural concerns about their long-windowed bodywork. However, many later vehicles were retained and led full lives, such as LA1249 (XUS 620S), an AN68A/1R from 1978, pictured with Strathclyde Transport in Argyle Street in 1995. (Courtesy of Phil Halewood)

Rossendale purchased three Alexander-bodied Atlanteans second-hand from Strathclyde PTE in 1984. One of these was No. 29 (HGG 243N) – an AN68/1R, new in 1975 to what was then Greater Glasgow PTE. The bus is pictured in Rawtenstall in March 1990.

Greater Manchester independent Stuart of Hyde purchased two Alexander-bodied AN68/1Rs from London Country North East in 1988. These had been part of a batch of thirty-one such vehicles, purchased previously by London Country from Strathclyde PTE. No. 106 (SGA 710N) is pictured on Piccadilly in Manchester in June 1992.

Short side windows are in evidence on this former Glasgow Alexander-bodied AN68/1R, operating with Keenan of Ayr. HGD 864L – new in 1973 – is pictured in Ayr town centre in September 1993, operating a shuttle service to the local Butlin's Wonderwest World holiday camp.

The location is outside York railway station in July 1997. Former Greater Glasgow PTE MDS 687P is pictured, converted to open-top, in service with Turner of York on sightseeing work. This Alexander-bodied AN68A/1R had been new in 1976.

Lancaster didn't take their first Atlanteans until the late 1970s, favouring long-wheelbase models with East Lancs bodywork. No. 206 (LFV 206X) – an AN68C/2R from 1981 – is pictured in the city's bus station in June 1991.

Lancaster, like several other north-west municipal fleets, took Atlanteans with East Lancs coach-style bodywork in the 1980s. Their No. 221 (BFV 221Y), pictured outside Lancaster's depot in Morecambe in June 1993, was one of three similar AN68D/2Rs new between 1983 and 1984.

A view inside Lancaster's garage and a rear-end shot of No. 223 (A223 MCK). This East Lancs-bodied AN68D/2R from 1984 had the distinction of being the very last Atlantean chassis to be bodied for the UK market. There were later registrations, however, featuring buses that had been in build on earlier chassis.

Single-deckers,
Non-PSV and Preserved

In the 1990s deregulated era, some operators had double-deck Atlanteans refurbished and rebodied as single-deckers, offering economy savings on the cost of purchasing a new bus. Nottingham City Transport had one of its AN68 examples so treated for its South Notts subsidiary in 1994. One East Lancs body replaced another in the transformation. It was subsequently re-registered RAU 804M when the original mark, OTO 555M, was transferred onto a newer Scania in the fleet. The Atlantean was eventually purchased by Derbyshire independent Hulley of Baslow, with whom it was photographed in Manchester's Heaton Park in September 2002.

A tender background romantic moment in South Shields in October 1995. However, the main interest is, of course, Hylton Castle (Catch-a-Bus) HIL 4349. This had originally been SUG 595M, a Roe-bodied AN68/2R double-decker, new to West Yorkshire PTE in 1974. The bus received this East Lancs single-deck body in 1992.

Another East Lancs single-deck rebody was Sheffield Omnibus No. 2501 (IIL 2501), pictured in Sheffield city centre in April 1996. This had started out as LJA 645P, a Northern Counties-bodied AN68A/1R, new to Greater Manchester PTE. Sheffield Omnibus initially purchased it from Hyndburn and operated in its original form for a while. Then the body was removed, with the chassis refurbished and lengthened, prior to the receipt of its new body.

Another rebodied example for Sheffield Omnibus was XRF 26S, which had originally been new to East Staffordshire in 1978. East Lancs once again did the honours in 1993, replacing one of their own double-deck bodies. The purchase of Sheffield Omnibus by Yorkshire Traction saw it transferred to Traction's Lincolnshire Road Car subsidiary. It's in this guise that it visited the Sandtoft Gathering in this shot from July 1999.

Fylde No. 5 (TKU 465K) was a PDR2/1 that began life as an Alexander-bodied double-decker with Bradford Corporation in 1971. Fylde had this and three other sister vehicles rebodied as single-deckers by Northern Counties in 1994. Blackpool's depressing Talbot Road bus station – mercifully since closed – is the location, in June 1994.

Park Royal-bodied AN68/1R XJA 534L was new to SELNEC PTE in 1973 as their No. 7134. It later passed to Greater Manchester PTE upon local government reorganisation in 1974; and, upon withdrawal at deregulation, was retained by the PTE as a publicity vehicle. This shot in Manchester's Piccadilly bus station in April 1989 demonstrates the rather dull two-tone grey and white livery employed.

The dismal surroundings of Manchester's Chorlton Street coach station in June 1989 provide the setting for Ribble TD8 (PCK 335) – a driver trainer in the fleet and a remarkable survivor. This early PDR1/1 with Metro-Cammell semi-lowbridge bodywork had been new in March 1961. Sadly, the bus no longer survives, but its registration has since graced numerous newer vehicles.

OBN 301H was numerically the last of fifteen PDR1A/1s ordered by Bolton Corporation but delivered to SELNEC PTE between late 1969 and early 1970. East Lancs built the dual-door bodywork to a highly distinctive style, featuring sloping windows. By the time of this shot in Manchester in March 1990, it had found a new role as a mobile help unit for the Trades Union Congress, promoting women's union rights.

UDT 181S, a former South Yorkshire PTE 1978 East Lancs-bodied AN68A/1R, is pictured at South Yorkshire Transport's Rotherham garage in August 1993. The bus had been converted to a mobile women's health unit, with its original front door panelled over and access through the remaining centre exit.

Another non-PSV, former SYPTE bus at Rotherham in August 1993 was XWG 630T – an AN68A/1R with Roe bodywork from 1978, which had been converted into a training vehicle by SYT. The removal of the staircase and the addition of extra side windows in its place can be clearly seen.

Central Manchester in January 1994, and MTL have drafted in this Alexander-bodied AN68/1R driver trainer from their main Merseybus fleet as they recruit drivers for their new MTL Manchester operation. No. 0682 (VWM 82L) was new to Southport Corporation in 1973, before that operator's takeover by Merseyside PTE the following year.

This Alexander-bodied PDR1A/1 was originally new to Edinburgh Corporation in 1970. In this view in August 1994, SSF 380H was in use as a children's play bus, its passenger-carrying days long over. The bus is pictured passing Edinburgh Zoo, on the outskirts of the city.

Alexander-bodied PDR2/1 XKC 835K is pictured in Chorlton Street, Manchester, in February 1995, in use with Sherenades Dance Troupe of Flixton. It had been new to Merseyside PTE in 1971, from an original order by Liverpool Corporation. It had spent time in the interim on the Isle of Man as MAN 5832. Its previous operator's livery and fleet number is still carried, together with a Manx advert.

In July 1995, Asda were recruiting staff in Manchester for a new superstore in Trafford Park. For this they hired No. A106 (LNA 166G) as a recruitment vehicle from GM Buses South. This Park Royal-bodied PDR2/1 had been new to Manchester City Transport in 1968 – one of its famous Mancunian class. After passing to SELNEC and then Greater Manchester PTE, it was converted to this format as *Exhibus* in the early 1980s. Piccadilly Gardens in central Manchester is the location.

In use as a toy library and play bus in Hartlepool in August 1995 was VFT 191T. This was a long AN68A/2R model with MCW bodywork that had been new to Tyne and Wear PTE in 1979.

A former Grampian Alexander-bodied AN68A/1R in use as a driver trainer. DSA 253T was an inter-group transfer by First from Aberdeen to their Greater Manchester fleet. A rainy Withy Grove in central Manchester is the location, in May 1997.

KPJ 245W was an AN68B/1R with Roe body, new to London Country in September 1980. It is captured nearly twenty-one years later in April 2001 in Chorlton Street, Manchester. The bus is being used as a mobile diner for film location work with The Big Diner Bus Company.

Another Atlantean in use as a film diner bus is URN 207V, owned by Jay-Bee, pictured in Manchester in February 2006. This East Lancs-bodied AN68A/2R had been new to Lancaster in December 1979.

Another former London Country Roe-bodied AN68B/1R is KPJ 284W, captured in use as a promotional vehicle for *Jobs and Training Weekly*. The bus is pictured in Quay Street in Manchester in March 2006, with the famous Opera House in the background.

Orange balloons and uniformed staff are still in evidence, but the day's work of promoting EasyJet is done for Alexander-bodied AN68/1R BFS 43L, as it moves away onto Piccadilly, Manchester, on 31 March 2008. The bus had gained the open-top conversion while with previous owners Lothian.

A rear-end shot to highlight the distinctive Atlantean engine cover and typical cut-away back window. The bus is UNA 777S, an AN68A/1R with Northern Counties body, new to Greater Manchester PTE in 1977. In this view in Rochdale in 2010, it is owned by Commbus as a mobile exhibition vehicle, in use on this occasion by the death and bereavement help group Dying Matters.

This Roe-bodied PDR2/1 has remained a familiar sight in Leeds over the years. New in 1971 to the city's transport department, DUA 473K plied the city streets under both Leeds and later West Yorkshire PTE ownership. Then, upon withdrawal, it was bought by the Leeds-based *Yorkshire Post,* who had it converted to a promotional vehicle with a partial open-top. A sunny day in September 2011 sees it parked up in the city centre.

The picturesque setting of Peak Rail at Rowsley, Derbyshire, in June 2019, with former Greater Manchester PTE AN68D/1R A671 HNB, in use as a play bus. This Northern Counties-bodied example had served out its last regular passenger-carrying days with North Birmingham Busways, before conversion to this non-PSV role.

Leyland's two Lowloader prototypes were the forerunners of what became the Atlantean. This is the second example – XTC 684 – with a Metro-Cammell body. This remarkable vehicle is now happily preserved and housed at the North West Transport Museum in St Helens. This view from September 1998 sees it parked outside the Leyland Museum at an event to mark the 40th anniversary of the first production Atlantean.

A familiar sight on the preservation scene is former Wallasey Corporation No. 1 (FHF 451) – the first production Atlantean to enter service when new in December 1958. This Metro-Cammell-bodied PDR1/1 is pictured at the head of a line of much newer Merseyside-themed Atlanteans, at a rally at the North West Vehicle Restoration Trust in Kirkby in June 2018.

Entering service a very short time after Wallasey No. 1 was Glasgow Corporation's No. LA1 (FYS 998) – an Alexander-bodied PDR1/1 and the first production Atlantean in Scotland. The bus has been in preservation since 1974, after a brief spell as a driver trainer the previous year. It is pictured in June 2019 in the impressive premises of the Glasgow Vintage Vehicle Trust, at the former bus garage at Bridgeton, to the east of the city. (Courtesy of Phil Halewood)

While Wallasey, Glasgow and others all had early examples in service, the actual first Atlantean chassis, numerically, were ten with Metro-Cammell bodies for Manchester Corporation. However, a union dispute over their usage meant they languished in storage, not entering service until April 1960. Local press at the time branded them 'Red Dragons'. No. 3629 (UNB 629) was later exported to Australia, before being repatriated for preservation. It now resides at Manchester's Museum of Transport – pictured here near the museum's premises in Cheetham in 2007.

One of the iconic bus designs of the 1960s was Manchester's Mancunian class – designed in-house by Ken Mortimer under the guidance of manager Ralph Bennett and bodied by various coachbuilders on Atlantean and Fleetline chassis. The first Atlantean example – Park Royal-bodied PDR1/1 1001 (HVM 901F) – is rightly preserved in the care of the Manchester Museum of Transport. The crisp styling and bright livery are much in evidence in this view in Heaton Park, Manchester, in 2012.

Before his stint at Manchester, Ralph Bennett was manager at Bolton and, while there, oversaw a similar transformation in livery application and vehicle design for that corporation's buses. Preserved Bolton No. 185 (UWH 185) – an East Lancs-bodied PDR1/1 from 1963 – is typical of this radical new look. It was captured looking extremely smart on a lovely summer's day in Blackpool in June 2010.

Another major operator who sought to break away from the rather austere, boxy designs of initial rear-engined buses was Liverpool. They specified a much fresher-looking design on several hundred Metro-Cammell-bodied Atlanteans, featuring peaked domes and sloping windows – a style that no doubt influenced East Lancs, and later Alexander, in their bodywork. Preserved No. L501 (501 KD) – new in 1962 – arrives at the Merseyside Transport Trust's premises in Burscough on a running day in July 2017.

Typical of early Atlanteans for the BET Group, is preserved PMT L9766 (766 EVT), a Weymann-bodied PDR1/1 from 1959, built to the semi-lowbridge layout. This has been a stalwart of the preservation scene for many years and looks very smart in this view in August 2010.

Oldham Corporation invested substantially in Atlanteans from 1965 until their takeover by SELNEC in 1969, taking PDR1/1 and PDR1A/1 models. This also included examples ordered by the corporation but delivered to SELNEC. The majority had bodywork by Roe to a distinctive design, which is demonstrated by preserved No. 163 (OBU 163F) from 1967, pictured at Peak Rail at Rowsley in June 2011.

Preserved former Bournemouth Corporation No. 170 (AEL 170B) is pictured at a wet bus rally at the Gladstone Pottery Museum in Longton, near Stoke-on-Trent, in August 2013. This smart 1964 PDR1/1 features a Weymann body with styling very heavily influenced by the Alexander design of the time.

Although the Atlantean was primarily a double-decker, several municipal operators specified single-deck bodies during the late 1960s and early 1970s. One such vehicle was GEX 740F, attractively preserved in the colours of Great Yarmouth Corporation in this view in Halifax in May 1994. This was one of three such Marshall-bodied PDR1/1s, new to them in 1968.

The gorgeous Newcastle-derived livery of cadmium yellow shines through on preserved Tyneside PTE 680 (GBB 516K). This PDR2/1 model from 1972 has Alexander dual-door bodywork, together with nearside staircase. The end of Boyle Street in Cheetham, Manchester, is the location in September 2007.

PDR1/1 657 BWB was new in 1962 to Sheffield Joint Omnibus Committee as their No. 1357, carrying a Weymann body. It was rebodied by Park Royal following major fire damage in 1968. After passing to South Yorkshire PTE in 1974 and a spell in the training fleet, No. 1357 was purchased for preservation and restored to its former JOC condition. Here the bus mingles with modern traffic in Sheffield in May 2013.

From the very first Glasgow Atlantean (featured a little earlier) to numerically the penultimate one to be delivered new to Glasgow and successors. Preserved No. LA1448 (CUS 302X) – an Alexander-bodied AN68A/1R – was new to Strathclyde PTE in October 1981. It has been in preservation since withdrawal by First Greater Glasgow in 1998 and is pictured in that identity, passing Glasgow's Riverside Museum, in October 2019.

Latecomers

Although Atlantean production ended in 1986, there were two further examples that were registered for UK service after that. Both had been intended for export, but, for different reasons, had never reached their intended destinations; and both were considerably older than their registration numbers would suggest.

D850 AVV was a 1980 Willowbrook-bodied AN68/2L, intended for export to Baghdad. Part of a larger batch of similar buses, it was damaged in transit and never reached Iraq. It remained unused in Leyland ownership until 1987, when it was acquired by Whippet of Fenstanton, converted to right-hand drive and taxed for the first time that October. It is pictured in Whippet's yard in May 1995. (Courtesy of Graham Ashworth)

The latest registered Atlantean in the UK was F212 JWV. It was also the only Atlantean to be bodied by Neoplan and was without doubt the oddest-looking example as a result. This AN68/2L was actually new in 1982, as part of an unsuccessful bid by Leyland to secure business in Saudi Arabia. It remained unregistered until October 1988 when it was bought by an Oxfordshire Christian group for use as an exhibition unit and branded *The King's Coach*. It is pictured later, in Wickford, Essex, in September 2012, still in its original left-hand drive layout. (Courtesy of Graham Ashworth)